Cambridge Discovery Readers

Level 3

Series editor: Nicholas Tims

Running Wild

Margaret Johnson

CAMBRIDGE
UNIVERSITY PRESS

CAMBRIDGE
UNIVERSITY PRESS

University Printing House, Cambridge CB2 8BS, United Kingdom

One Liberty Plaza, 20th Floor, New York, NY 10006, USA

477 Williamstown Road, Port Melbourne, VIC 3207, Australia

314–321, 3rd Floor, Plot 3, Splendor Forum, Jasola District Centre, New Delhi – 110025, India

103 Penang Road, #05-06/07, Visioncrest Commercial, Singapore 238467

Cambridge University Press is part of the University of Cambridge.

It furthers the University's mission by disseminating knowledge in the pursuit of education, learning and research at the highest international levels of excellence.

www.cambridge.org

This American English edition is based on *Running Wild*, ISBN 978-84-832-3501-0 first published by Cambridge University Press in 2009.

First published 2009
American English edition 2010

20 19 18 17 16 15 14 13 12 11 10 9 8 7 6 5 4

Printed in Great Britain by CPI Group (UK) Ltd, Croydon CR0 4YY

ISBN 978-0-521-14901-3 Paperback American English edition

Illustrations by Raúl Allen (c/o Pencil Illustradoes)

Audio recording by hyphen

Exercises by Peter McDonnell

The publishers are grateful to the following for permission to reproduce photographic material:

© Eric Gevaert | Dreamstime.com and © Jon Helgason | Dreamstime.com for cover image

Contents

People in the story

Luke Robinson: a fourteen-year-old boy
Alex Brown: also fourteen; Luke's neighbor
Jet: a black panther
Mrs. Robinson: Luke's mother
Mrs. Brown: Alex's mother
Mr. Clark: one of Luke's teachers

BEFORE YOU READ

● ●

1 Look at *People in the story* and the pictures in the first two chapters. Answer the question.

Which characters are in these first two chapters?

....

Chapter 1

The phone

It was a gray Sunday afternoon, and I was walking through the park with my neighbor Alex. Alex had a big stick and he was hitting trees with it. The stick made a THWACK sound when it hit the trees.

"It's so boring around here," Alex said. THWACK! "Nothing ever happens." *THWACK!*

"It'll be vacation soon," I said.

"So what?" Alex said. "Vacation is boring, too." He threw the stick into the air as hard as he could. When it came down it almost hit a man who was walking past with his dog.

"Hey, kid!" shouted the man. "Be more careful!"

Alex laughed. He picked up the stick and threw it again.

"Hey, come here!" the man shouted.

"Why should I?" Alex said.

The man began to come over. He was big as well as angry.

"Let's go!" I said to Alex.

The man began to move toward Alex. We started to run, with Alex laughing all the way. When it was safe to stop, we sat on a wall for a rest. Alex was still laughing.

"Did you see the size of him?" he asked. "Fat pig."

A woman came toward us. She had two young children and a baby. Suddenly one of the children fell over. He began to scream loudly.

"Oh, Jack!" the woman said. She sounded tired. "Wait there," she said to the other child. Then she put her bag down on the ground so she could help the little boy up.

"Come on, Jack," she said. "You're all right."

Alex got down from the wall. He looked at me quickly. I started to get down from the wall. Then Alex began to run over to the woman and her children. I thought he was going to help them or something, but he didn't. He reached into the woman's bag and took something out.

The woman turned around and saw him.

"My phone!" she shouted. "They took my phone!"

Alex looked at me. "Come on!" he said. "Run!"

I could run faster than Alex. Soon I was in front of him. I ran right across the park and through the trees until I reached a building. It was the park restrooms. I ran behind them and stopped.

"Luke?" Alex called, following me. "What did you come down here for?" His face was red. He looked as hot as I felt.

"To hide," I said.

"It smells," he said.

I didn't answer. I didn't like the smell either. I could think of lots of places I would rather be, like at home waiting for Mom to get back from work. Even school would be better than this, though I'd never tell Alex that. Alex hated school and thought anyone who liked it was crazy.

I still couldn't believe what Alex had done.

"Wasn't that great?" he laughed now, his face alive as he remembered.

"Shh!" I said. "I can hear someone coming."

Alex gave me an angry look. His face could change so quickly. Light to dark. Sun to rain.

"It won't be *her*, Luke," he said. "She couldn't run after us with all those kids to watch." He stood up. "Come on. Let's get out of here. It smells awful." And he began to walk down the side of the restroom toward the street.

I followed him slowly. I thought we should hide for longer. The woman might tell the police. When I reached Alex, he was playing with the woman's phone. He had forgotten about the smell from the restrooms.

"I can't think of any numbers to call!" Alex said, looking down at the phone.

I put my hands in my pockets and stood by the restroom entrance, waiting for him. I couldn't get the woman's face out of my head. I felt sorry for her. I was worried, too. She said "*they*" took my phone. I couldn't stop and say "I didn't take it! It wasn't me!" So I had to run and hide with Alex. What if we saw the woman again? Or if she told the police what we looked like?

"Don't you know any numbers?" Alex was saying angrily to me now.

I knew Mom's number, but I wasn't telling Alex that.

"No, sorry," I said. I thought Alex would probably throw the phone down soon. He used to get mad and throw his toys across the room when we were young children. He hasn't changed much.

It was raining now and I just wanted to go home. I wished Alex didn't live next door to me. But it was better to be Alex's friend. I'd seen what he was like to people who weren't his friends.

Suddenly it began to rain harder. Alex pushed the phone into his pocket.

"Come on," he said to me angrily, as if the bad weather and not having any numbers to call were all my fault.

And at last we began to walk toward home.

Chapter 2

Escape

Twenty kilometers away Jet was waiting, too. Jet was a wild cat – a black panther. The man who kept her had bought her as a baby. But now Jet was an adult – a big adult cat that hated the dark wooden house the man kept her in. It smelled and very little light got in, except for when the man opened the door to throw her food in.

Sometimes, at night, Jet dreamed of a different type of light, the type of light that comes through forest trees. Dark, light; dark, light; changing all the time, as a panther walks quietly toward the sounds of life and her next meal.

When she was awake, Jet quickly forgot about her dreams. There was an old metal cage inside her wooden house. She walked up and down in this cage for hours. Sometimes she got angry and threw herself at the old metal. Sometimes she was so angry she made a lot of noise. She roared[1] and roared until her throat[2] hurt. There was no one to hear her. The man was out at work all day and the house was in the middle of the countryside. Nobody ever came to help her and afterward, Jet always fell into a hopeless sleep on the dirty floor.

But that evening, everything was different. That evening Jet was waiting for more than the old meat the man threw into her house before he went inside his house for the night. That evening, Jet was waiting to escape.

At last, Jet heard the sound of a door opening and closing. The man was coming. Jet lay quietly, listening as he walked toward her house. The metal cage was old and weak. Earlier that day, when Jet had thrown herself against it, something had broken. And now Jet wasn't in the cage anymore. She was out in the wooden house, waiting for the door to open. She was ready to jump.

The man stopped outside the wooden house. Jet didn't move a millimeter. She was listening for the sound of the key in the lock. At last it came. Without making any noise at all, Jet moved even closer to the door. The key turned. The door began to open.

The man still had the meat in his hand when Jet jumped. As her sharp teeth closed on his neck, the meat dropped onto the dirty ground.

It was an almost soundless kill. Jet had never killed a living thing before, but she still knew just what to do. Her teeth held on tight[3] and then she shook the man. Once, twice. By the third time, he was dead.

Jet was hungry, but she didn't stop to eat. She dropped the man on the ground next to the meat and then she ran quickly away, keeping to the dark places away from the late evening sun. She ran past the man's house and up the road toward the woods. Inside the woods, she disappeared into the darkness.

The man had lived alone. He didn't have any friends or family. So it was the mailman who found the body a week later, when he drove up to the house with the man's phone bill.

But, by then, Jet had gone.

LOOKING BACK

1 Check your answer to *Before you read* on page 4.

ACTIVITIES

2 Complete the sentences with the names in the box.

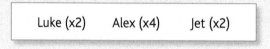

| Luke (x2) | Alex (x4) | Jet (x2) |

1   *Luke* tells the story in Chapter 1.
2   .... is bored with life.
3   .... wants to be free.
4   .... doesn't like school.
5   .... is very strong and dangerous.
6   .... gets angry very easily.
7   .... enjoys doing bad things.
8   .... doesn't like trouble.

3 <u>Underline</u> the correct words in each sentence.
1   The woman with the phone has *two / three* children.
2   The boy begins to cry because *he falls over / Alex steals the phone*.
3   Luke thinks that Alex is going to *steal the mother's phone / help the mother*.
4   *Alex / Luke* runs faster than his friend.
5   Luke *is / isn't* happy that Alex stole the phone.
6   Alex is *the same as / different from* when he was a child.
7   Jet often dreams about *light / her next meal*.
8   This *is / isn't* the first time Jet has killed.
9   The man lives *with his family / on his own*.

4 What do the <u>underlined</u> words refer to in these lines from the text?

1 "Did you see the size of <u>him</u>?" (page 6) *the man in the car*

2 "<u>They</u> took my phone!" (page 7) ....

3 "It won't be <u>her</u>, Luke," he said. (page 8) ....

4 "Why won't <u>it</u> work?" (page 8) ....

5 Earlier that day, when Jet had thrown herself against <u>it</u>, something had broken. (page 11) ....

6 As <u>her</u> sharp teeth closed on his neck (page 13)

....

5 Answer the questions.

1 Why does Alex steal the cell phone?

Because everything is boring.

2 Why does Luke hide with Alex?

....

3 How long have Alex and Luke been friends?

....

4 Why is Jet unhappy?

....

5 Where does Jet go when she escapes?

....

LOOKING FORWARD

•••

6 Check (✓) what you think happens in the next two chapters.

1 Luke and Alex meet Jet and have an adventure. ☐

2 Jet kills again. ☐

Chapter 3

Ridge Woods

"I'm going out straight after work tonight," Mom told me at breakfast the next morning.

She was smoking her first cigarette of the day. I hated her smoking, but I said nothing. I just continued eating my toast.

"It's Maria's fortieth birthday," Mom continued.

I wasn't interested. I didn't like Maria or any of Mom's

other friends from her new job. They wore short skirts and too much makeup. Mom was better than that.

"Don't look at me like that, Luke," Mom told me now. "I need to go out with my friends sometimes. I can't just sit in the house night after night. Half of the time you're out anyway."

I still didn't speak and Mom pushed her coffee away and got up from the table. I knew she was mad at me. She thought I was difficult.

She picked up her bag and went to the door.

"Remember to do your homework tonight," she said.

I heard the front door open and close, and the sound of her shoes going click clack down the steps to the street. It was too late to say goodbye now.

I felt fed up as I put my school books into my bag. What did I want from Mom anyway? She was right; she did need to go out sometimes. I went to a private school, and Mom worked very hard to pay for it. She did it for me – she wanted me to have the best education. And I wasn't a little kid anymore. I hadn't been a little kid for a long time, not since before Dad died.

Alex came out of his house at the same time as me. He did it so often I sometimes thought he must wait by the window until he saw me come out. Except that waiting by a window for people wasn't the type of thing someone like Alex did.

Alex doesn't really have a dad either, or at least not very often. Alex's dad is a businessman and he's often away on business somewhere around the world. Alex's mom doesn't work like mine does, so Alex sees more of her. Not that he wants to – Alex doesn't like his mom. They're always arguing. I could hear her shouting out of the door to him now.

"And come straight home tonight! Your Uncle Rob's coming for dinner."

She came to the door and saw me.

"Oh, hello, Luke," she said.

"Morning, Mrs. Brown," I said, smiling. I don't know why I was able to be nice to her when I hadn't been nice to my own mom.

She gave me a smile.

"Make sure he comes straight back after school please, Luke."

As if I could make Alex do anything he didn't want to! I wasn't surprised when he laughed the minute the front door closed on his mother.

"Let's go up to Ridge Woods tonight," he said.

I looked at him.

"What about your uncle?" I asked.

"What about him?" Alex said. And that was the end of the conversation.

* * *

Ridge Woods has been a playground for Alex and me for years. It's an area of grass and trees just outside the city, not far from where we live. People go there to walk their dogs.

When Alex and I were younger, we used to go there to climb trees or make tree houses with pieces of old wood. It was fun to go up there in the winter when it snowed, too.

Now that we're older, Alex and I still go up there to have fun; it's just a different type of fun. It's nice to be up there among the trees, away from everybody. I like trees and animals. I have always liked them. I like seeing the first leaves in the spring and hearing all the different bird songs.

Alex used to like those things too, but he doesn't seem to care about them anymore. These days, he prefers to throw rocks at the trees or sit around smoking a cigarette.

Sometimes he talks to me about things, too – his dad being away so much, for example. But he hasn't talked about his dad for a while now and I don't like to ask him about it. It's getting harder to know what to talk to Alex about these days.

Alex was quiet that evening when we went up to Ridge

Woods after school. I guessed[4] it might be something to do with his Uncle Rob coming to dinner. I knew Rob wasn't Alex's real uncle – he was a friend of Alex's dad. He came to see Alex's mom and Alex a lot. Alex didn't like him.

It was the last week of school before summer vacation. The sun was shining and it was really warm. When Alex and I got to the top of the hill, we took our sweaters off and lay down, looking at the sky. We'd come up here at night a few times to look at the stars. It was excellent.

After a while, Alex sat up and I heard him light a cigarette. I hate smoking. Smoking killed my dad. He smoked all his life and then he died from cancer.

Alex tried to make me smoke once; we had a real fight about it – bloody noses and everything. But when my dad died, I decided I was never going to smoke. And I never have.

"Everything's so boring," Alex said suddenly, picking grass with his free hand and throwing it up in the air.

I watched the grass fall.

"Why can't something happen?" Alex said and he took a stick and began to hit the grass with it. His cigarette fell to the ground next to some dead leaves. I picked it up and held it out to him so that the leaves wouldn't catch fire. The ground was very dry.

"Careful," I said. "You might start a fire."

Alex smiled as he took the cigarette from me.

"Now that's a good idea," he said. He reached into his school bag for a lighter. "Let's burn this place down!" he said.

Chapter 4

Hiding

Jet reached Ridge Woods in the night. She found a place to hide among the trees – a place where people didn't walk with their dogs. She was tired, so she slept for a few hours. When she woke, she was hungry.

Very carefully, Jet began to walk toward the grassy area beyond the trees. She waited, still hidden by the trees, and looked out. Nothing moved. She smelled the air and knew that animals were somewhere close by under the ground. If she was patient, they would soon come out from their holes.

They did. Jet caught a young rabbit and ate it quickly. She was still hungry. But now the other animals knew Jet was there and they were staying under the ground. She didn't eat again that night.

Jet thought about leaving the trees to look for more food. But when she smelled the air, she was afraid. She could smell people. And when she smelled people, she remembered the man.

She could smell something else, too. And she could see a strange orange light in the trees beyond the grassy place. Jet didn't know what the smell or the orange light was, but everything in her told her that it was dangerous. So, still feeling hungry, Jet turned and walked away from the grass and back into the darkness of the trees.

LOOKING BACK

1 Check your answer to *Looking forward* on page 15.

ACTIVITIES

2 Put the sentences in order.

1 Alex and Luke take off their sweaters. ☐
2 Luke's mom goes to work. ☐1☐
3 Alex comes out of his house. ☐
4 Alex and Luke go to Ridge Woods. ☐
5 Luke puts his school books in his bag. ☐
6 Alex's cigarette falls to the ground. ☐
7 Alex's mom comes to the door. ☐
8 Alex says he wants to go to Ridge Woods after school. ☐

3 Match the two parts of the sentences.

1 Luke's mom is going out ☐e☐
2 Luke's mom works hard ☐
3 Alex's mom wants him to come home ☐
4 Alex takes a lighter ☐
5 The animals stay ☐
6 Jet hides ☐

a after school.
b from his school bag.
c in the darkness.
d at her job.
e after work.
f under the ground.

4 Are the sentences true (*T*) or false (*F*)?
1 Alex's dad isn't home very often. ☐*T*
2 Alex and his mom argue a lot. ☐
3 Alex's mom has a job. ☐
4 Jet eats two rabbits. ☐
5 The animals hide from Jet. ☐

5 Answer the questions.
1 Why is Alex's dad often away from home?

....

2 What did Luke and Alex do in Ridge Woods when they were children?

....

3 Who is Rob?

....

4 Why doesn't Luke like smoking?

....

5 What is the "strange orange light" that Jet sees?

....

LOOKING FORWARD

6 Answer the questions.
1 Luke's teacher wants to speak to him. What do you think he says?

....

2 Jet is very hungry. What do you think she eats?

....

3 Luke finds something in Ridge Woods. What do you think it is?

....

Chapter 5

Teacher talk

At school the next day, Mr. Clark, my English teacher, spoke to me at the end of the last class. "Luke Robinson," he said. "Can you stay behind, please?"

I could feel everyone looking at me as they hurried out of the classroom. I didn't look at Alex.

"Sit down, Luke," Mr. Clark said kindly after everyone had gone.

I pulled a chair out from behind a desk. It made a loud sound on the hard wood floor. I sat down and looked at the floor – anywhere but at Mr. Clark's kind face.

"Luke," Mr. Clark said, "I asked you to stay behind today because your work hasn't been as good lately. And you don't always seem to be listening in class."

He waited. I didn't know if he wanted me to say sorry or if he was just waiting for me to explain. I didn't do either.

"Luke," Mr. Clark said, trying again. "Is everything all right? If anything's wrong, you can always tell me, you know."

I thought about the fire of the day before – orange tongues of fire reaching up to the sky, burning leaves sending smoke up into the air. I remembered Alex laughing and screaming and dancing, his face alive with happiness. I remembered worrying about the rabbits that might die. I didn't want the whole[5] woods to burn and I felt completely helpless and useless. I was so happy when I heard the sound of the fire engine and Alex shouted "Run!" at me.

"No," I said to Mr. Clark. "There's nothing wrong."

Mr. Clark looked tired. I knew he didn't believe me.

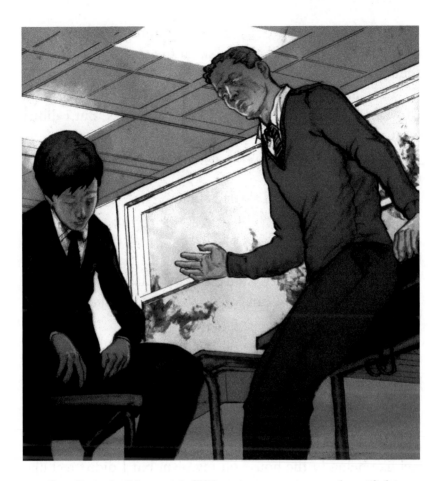

"Well, Luke," he said, "I'll write to your mother if things don't change. I don't want to have to do that. I know things haven't been easy since your father died."

Mr. Clark waited for me to speak again, but I couldn't. I hadn't expected him to talk about Dad and I knew I might cry if I tried to say anything now. I'm usually OK at talking about Dad these days, but not if people surprise me with it.

"You used to love writing," Mr. Clark was saying now. I wanted him to stop talking. I just wanted to escape and be on my own. "I still remember a piece you wrote about the trees and flowers in Ridge Woods. It was very good. When you read it to the class, we could almost smell the smells and hear the sounds."

I remembered the piece of writing he was talking about. I'd written about how I felt about Ridge Woods. But I didn't want to write about how I felt lately.

"What's changed, Luke?" Mr. Clark asked. "Don't you enjoy writing now?"

He waited again and at last I spoke.

"I just can't do it anymore, sir," I said.

"Look, Luke," Mr. Clark said, "this is none of my business, but have you tried writing about your dad? It might help."

I suddenly felt angry. I looked at Mr. Clark.

"No," I said. "Look, can I go now, sir? Mom asked me to be home on time."

Mr. Clark looked tired again. "All right, Luke," he said. "You can go. But remember what I said. I want you to do your homework on time and I want you to listen in class."

"Yes, sir," I said and then I left.

I hadn't told Mr. Clark the truth. Mom hadn't asked me to come straight home. She was working late tonight. I didn't feel like being in the house on my own, but I didn't feel like meeting up with Alex either. I knew he would be waiting for me at the school entrance, so I didn't go that way. I walked across the parking lot and climbed over a wall. Then I began to walk toward Ridge Woods.

Chapter 6

An unlucky dog

Jet was beginning to get used to her new home. Sometimes, when the sun came through the leaves, it was almost like the forests of her dreams. The strange orange light that had worried her had gone now. She was still hungry though. She'd caught a few more rabbits, but the others had gotten frightened and moved away. She would have to follow them soon if she wanted to eat. There were only mice and small birds here, but she needed more.

Something held her back though. There were people around. Nobody had come close to where she was hiding, but she could still smell them. So, for now, she stayed where she was, in the trees. She tried to sleep so she wouldn't think about being hungry.

Suddenly something woke her. A man's voice.

"Westy! Here, boy! Westy!" The man was standing on the grass. He was calling toward Jet's trees.

Without a sound, Jet moved farther back into the darkness.

"Westy! Where are you, boy?" The man's voice was quieter now; he was moving away.

But just as Jet began to lie down again, there was another sound. Something was moving quickly toward her, its feet noisy on the carpet of old leaves. An animal. Jet got ready to jump. The animal didn't see her coming. It died without making any sound at all.

As Jet began to eat, she could hear the man shouting out in the field.

"Westy! Westy!"

Chapter 7

Eyes

When I reached Ridge Woods, I went straight up the hill to where Alex had started the fire. I felt sick looking at it. Everything was black – the trees were all burned, the grass was all burned. Yesterday this had been a beautiful place, but now it was ugly and black and dead. And it smelled awful.

Standing there, looking at it, I remembered the conversation I had just had with Mr. Clark. If I wrote about this, I would use words like "war" and "death" and "crime." Ugly words. Angry words. But words wouldn't bring the trees and the grass back to life.

A couple[6] came up the hill with their two dogs.

"Hello," they said to me. "Isn't this awful?"

"Yes," I said. But I couldn't look at them and soon they walked away. When I looked at them, they were talking. I knew what they were saying.

"Do you think he did it? Maybe we should call the police."

Quickly, I began to walk down the hill, away from the blackness. My head hurt and I felt so angry I wanted to scream and shout. If Alex had suddenly come out from the trees, I would have run at him and hit him. Dad had taught me never to hit anyone, but Dad was dead. He had left me here and now I had to make my own decisions.

Suddenly a man spoke.

"Excuse me."

I jumped. I hadn't known the man was there.

"You haven't seen my dog anywhere, have you? He's a little

white terrier. His name's Westy."

The man was looking worried. I shook my head.

"No, sorry," I said. "I haven't seen him."

"I've been looking for over an hour now," the man said. "He just seemed to disappear."

"Sorry," I said again.

The man tried to smile.

"Oh," he said. "I'm sure I'll find him by dinnertime. He likes to eat. If you do see him, can you call me? He's wearing a collar around his neck. My phone number is on it."

"Yes, all right," I said. "I'll look out for him."

"Thanks a lot," the man said and then he left.

As he walked away, I heard him calling his dog.

"Westy! Westy! Come on, boy!"

I kept going down the hill, looking to the left and to the right for the dog. It gave me something to do – something to stop me from thinking about how angry I was. Once I saw something white in the trees but, when I got closer, I saw it was only a plastic shopping bag.

I reached a grassy area where children play soccer. Some boys were about to start a game. They were from my school – they were wearing the school uniform. I like soccer, but I didn't feel like playing it today. So I left the grassy area and

went into the trees. The trees grew close together here and it was pretty dark. The leaves cut out the sky above my head. Suddenly there was a loud noise and I stopped. Maybe I had frightened an animal away or something. Something large had run off into the trees anyway. It had made a lot of noise – too much noise to be the man's dog. What was his name again? Westy. That was it. Maybe it was a deer. Or maybe a large dog.

I walked on. Behind me, I could still hear the boys shouting to each other as they enjoyed their game. "To me!" "Over here!" "Shoot!" They sounded happy and it made me feel alone. I felt as if I had a great big angry weight on my back. I didn't want to feel that way. I wanted to be able to run and shout and have fun just like them.

Suddenly, I saw something on the ground up ahead. It was something white. As I got closer, I could see it was animal fur – soft white animal fur. I looked down and saw that there was blood on it. Something else caught my eye, lying on the ground not far away. It was a collar with a little name tag.

I picked it up to read the name on the name tag, even though I already knew what it would say. Westy.

I stepped backward, suddenly afraid. Something had killed and eaten Westy. But what?

I remembered the animal I had frightened away as I had walked into the woods. What had it been? A deer wouldn't kill a dog and dogs didn't usually kill each other. Not unless[7] they're dangerous. Perhaps I shouldn't be in here. It might not be safe.

I'm not sure why I didn't run away immediately. I knew I should go home and call Westy's owner and the police. But I didn't. I walked farther into the trees, still holding Westy's collar. And that's when I saw the eyes. Dangerous eyes. Hungry eyes. Looking straight at me from the darkness of the trees.

I looked into those eyes for what seemed like half a lifetime and then I turned and I ran.

LOOKING BACK

• •

1 Check your answers to *Looking forward* on page 25.

ACTIVITIES

• •

2 <u>Underline</u> the correct words in each sentence.
1 Luke *looks / <u>doesn't look</u>* at Mr. Clark's face.
2 Mr. Clark speaks to Luke about *his writing / Ridge Woods burning*.
3 Luke's mom is *going out / working late* tonight.
4 Now Jet is afraid of *people / the strange orange light*.
5 Luke feels sick because *Ridge Woods was burned /
the people were talking about him*.
6 The last thing Luke finds is a *plastic bag / dog's collar*.
7 Luke *thinks / doesn't think* the noise in the woods was a deer.
8 Luke *calls / doesn't call* Westy's owner.

3 Complete the sentences with the names in the box.

Mr. Clark (x2)   Westy's owner   Luke (x3)   Alex   Jet

1 ...*Mr. Clark*... is Luke's English teacher.
2 .... 's work hasn't been as good as usual recently.
3 .... was happy when Ridge Woods burned.
4 .... thinks that Luke can write well.
5 .... doesn't want to be on his own at home.
6 .... can smell people.
7 .... is worried about his dog.
8 .... finds a dog's collar.

4 Are the sentences true (*T*) or false (*F*)?

1 Mr. Clark is going to write to Luke's mother. [F]
2 Luke still feels sad about his dad. ☐
3 Mr. Clark says that Luke should write about Ridge Woods again. ☐
4 Luke lies to Mr. Clark. ☐
5 Jet ate some rabbits. ☐
6 Westy dies quickly. ☐
7 Luke doesn't like playing soccer. ☐
8 Luke runs away when he finds the name tag. ☐

5 Answer the questions.

1 What does Mr. Clark think Luke's problem is?

2 How has Ridge Woods changed since the fire?

3 Why does Luke look for the dog?

4 What happened to Westy?

5 What exactly does Luke see in the trees at the end of Chapter 7?

LOOKING FORWARD

6 Check (✓) what you think happens in the next three chapters.

1 Luke goes to look for Jet again. ☐
2 Alex starts another fire. ☐

Chapter 8

Playing detective

"What happened to you yesterday afternoon?" Alex asked me on the way to school the next day.

Right away, I remembered the eyes. I have never, *ever* been so afraid in all my life. Just remembering it now, I felt afraid. As I ran wildly back the way I had come, toward the shouts of the boys playing soccer, I truly thought I was about to die. I expected the animal to run up behind me. To jump. To hold me down on the ground while its teeth bit into me.

"How long did Clarky keep you back for?" Alex asked.

I looked at him, not understanding at first. Then I realized what he was talking about: Mr. Clark – my conversation with Mr. Clark at school. And I remembered that Alex didn't know about the eyes in the trees. Or Westy. He didn't even know I'd been up in Ridge Woods. And Westy's owner didn't know I'd found Westy's fur and collar. Westy's collar was in a box under my bed. I'd kept it to give to his owner, but I hadn't called him yet.

Alex was looking at me strangely.

"Are you all right?" he asked. "You look as if you've been in a fight."

I put my hand up to my face. I had cut it running

through the trees the afternoon before. I'd been so afraid I hadn't looked where I was going. I'd just looked at the grass and the soccer players ahead. I told myself that, if only I could get there, I would be safe. I ran out of the woods like a crazy person. The boys had stopped their soccer game to look at me strangely.

Alex was looking at me like that now.

"No," I said, doing my best to make my voice sound normal. "I just fell over, that's all."

Alex was losing interest. He started to walk away. "See you later," he said.

But I had no plans to see Alex later. When school ended, I left the same way I had the evening before – across the parking lot and over the wall. Then I ran straight up to Ridge Woods.

*   *   *

Mom likes watching shows about police and detectives on TV. Sometimes I stay up late to watch them with her. I used to watch movies about the Wild West with Dad, too. I know all about looking on the ground to see where people and animals have been walking. If the ground isn't too dry, they can leave tracks where they walk. In movies about the Wild West, a man often looks at horse tracks and says, "he rode this way two hours ago."

Alex and I used to play Wild West games when we were younger. We made tracks in the ground with our feet and we hid behind trees or walls. We chased each other and we "killed" each other with our toy guns. "Bang[8], bang! You're dead!"

It was animal tracks I was interested in now and this time it was no game. As I went into the trees where I had seen the eyes, I knew that this time there would be no Alex jumping out with his toy gun and laughing. There was just me and whatever I had seen last night.

39

The ground was never completely dry under the trees. They stopped the sun from getting through and drying it out. I knew I would find some animal tracks if I looked closely.

This time I was very careful as I walked. I looked all around me and listened very hard for any sounds. There weren't many, except for the birds. There were no soccer players on the grass that afternoon and no dog walkers either.

It took me a few minutes to find the right place – the trees all looked the same. Then I saw something white ahead and I knew I had found Westy's fur again. When I got there, I picked it up and looked at it. On my way over here, I had seen a piece of paper on a tree. It was a poster asking if anybody had seen Westy.

Lost since Wednesday. Westy, a small white terrier dog. Much loved pet. $30 paid for information. Call Phil Bentley 240-571-0871.

That was a lot of money to me. But I wasn't ready to make any phone calls just yet.

I began to search the ground for animal tracks. I quickly found some. Something very large had stood right where I was now. Something had stood here to kill and eat Westy.

We've had a few cats over the years and a dog once, so I know the difference between cat tracks and dog tracks. It wasn't a dog that had stood here enjoying an unexpected dinner; it was a cat. Without question. Only it was a big cat – a *very* big cat. A cat that was big enough to kill a fourteen-year-old boy …

Chapter 9

The plan

I stood up straight to look around me again, listening so hard my ears almost hurt. But there was nothing. No, that isn't exactly true. I couldn't *see* anything and I couldn't *hear* anything, but ... Well, somehow I knew I wasn't alone. The animal was nearby. Hiding. Watching me.

The hairs on the back of my neck stood up. My mouth was dry. It was time to go.

This time I didn't run. I knew now that running had been a stupid thing to do. I've seen enough shows about wild animals to know that killers like a chase.

My heart was loud in my chest[9] as I walked quickly back through the trees and across the grass. I didn't even really feel safe when I reached the path[10] up the hill again. So, when I saw Alex sitting on a wooden seat, I was almost happy. At first.

When he saw me, Alex didn't smile.

"What are you doing here?" he asked.

He turned away and I saw he had a small knife. He was using it to cut into the seat.

"Nothing," I said.

"I waited for you at school," Alex said.

His voice sounded normal, but there was something angry about the way he was using the knife.

I wasn't sure what to say, so I said nothing. Alex turned to look at me.

"Where were you?" he asked.

"I came straight up here," I said.

He looked at me for a while. It was difficult to look back at him, but I didn't want to look at the knife either.

He turned away again.

"Did you see the place where we burned the trees down?" he asked.

We. My face turned red. I hadn't had anything to do with the fire; it had all been Alex. But that was just like Alex. Changing history.

"Yes," I said. "I saw."

Alex turned to me with a big smile.

"Great, isn't it?"

He got up and I saw the word he had cut into the seat. *Luke.* My face went red again, but I didn't say anything.

"Let's do it again!" Alex said. "Let's start another fire."

"No," I said. "I've got to get back." And I began to walk past him.

He put his hand out to stop me.

"What's wrong?" he asked. "Are you afraid?"

He was holding my arm. I couldn't move.

"No," I said. "I've just got to get back. Mom … wants to talk to me about something."

My arm was hurting. I didn't think Alex was going to let go. His eyes were cold. I've seen him look at other kids like that lots of times. Just before he hits them.

"Go on then, mama boy," he said at last, giving me a big push.

I fell over, face down in the dirt. Alex thought that was very funny. He was still laughing as I stood up and tried to get the dirt off my pants with my hand.

"Mommy's going to be very mad at you when you get home," he said in a baby voice. "She'll put you to bed without any supper."

I was so mad it felt like all my blood was in my head. "I hate you, Alex Brown," I thought. "I hate you."

*   *   *

"Mom?"

"I'm upstairs. In the bedroom."

I was so happy to hear Mom's voice when I got home. I didn't feel like being on my own. I ran upstairs to see her.

She was sitting on the bed, brushing her hair. She had her best dress on; clearly, she was going out.

"Are you OK?" She looked at me in the mirror.

"Yeah. Where are you going?" I asked, throwing down my school bag and sitting down on her bed.

"Out to dinner," she said. "And don't look at me like that. If you didn't keep going up to Ridge Woods after school, we'd get to see each other a little more often. I have no idea what you find to do up there."

I didn't answer. I thought Mom looked really nice. Something told me she was meeting a man for dinner, for a date. Mom's not old and Dad died three years ago now. I knew it should be OK for Mom to go out on a date, but it didn't feel OK. I didn't want her to forget about Dad and I didn't want her to go out anywhere. I wanted her to stay in with me and watch TV.

Mom got up.

"Your dinner's in the oven[11]," she said. "Pizza. Your favorite."

I still didn't answer and she tried again. "I tell you what," she said, "let's get a DVD out tomorrow, OK? You think about what you'd like to see and we'll go to the store. We could get some hamburgers, too."

"Tonight." I said. "Let's do it tonight."

"I can't tonight, Luke," Mom said.

"Please."

"No," she said and she sounded a little impatient with me now. I saw her looking at her watch. "I told you. I have plans tonight. We'll do it tomorrow, OK? Now, I've got to go. I won't be back late. Be good."

She kissed her fingers and pressed them to the top of my head and then she went downstairs. I heard her pick up her keys and her bag and then I heard the sound of the front door opening and closing.

After Mom had gone, I lay back on her bed and thought about the big cat. I'd only seen its eyes, so I didn't know what it looked like. Was it black or gold? A he or a she? I decided it was a she; I don't know why. I didn't really know anything about it. Except that it was alone, just like me.

The cat's tracks had shown that it was a large animal. I knew from the way it had killed that it was dangerous. But I thought it must still feel afraid. Ridge Woods has lots of trees, but it's really close to the city and lots of people go there. Big cats don't usually live so close to people; she wouldn't feel comfortable about that. It wasn't safe up there for her either. If she killed any more dogs, people would know something was wrong. They would search Ridge Woods and find the tracks just like I had. Then they would try to catch her. Or even to kill her.

The cat needed a friend. She could have killed me, but she didn't. Maybe she had wanted *me* to be her friend. I really wanted to help her, but I just didn't know how.

I lay there on Mom's bed, thinking about it for ages. When I finally went downstairs and opened the oven, the pizza was burned. I threw it away and looked in the fridge to see what else there was to eat. There was nothing quick; just meat and vegetables. I picked up the meat and looked at it. And suddenly I knew what I had to do.

Chapter 10

No escape

Jet knew she had to leave Ridge Woods. There were too many people around and no more animals had come her way. She was hungry again.

She waited until darkness fell before she left the safety of the trees. The moon was behind thick cloud; it was a very dark night. Nobody was around to see her make her way across the grass.

She stood for a while, trying to decide which way to go. The smell of people was too strong. She only knew she couldn't go back toward the man. He was dead; she had killed him, but there might be others like him.

Jet began to walk down the hill, away from the grass. As she walked, the light began to change, becoming more and more orange. Jet didn't like it. The smell of people was stronger here than ever.

She turned back the way she had come. Suddenly there was a loud noise. Jet stopped, ready to turn and run. The noise grew louder. Then two lights, as white as two bright[12] moons, came through the darkness toward her. Afraid, Jet ran back into the trees to hide.

There was nowhere safe and she was still hungry.

LOOKING BACK

• •

1 Check your answer to *Looking forward* on page 37.

ACTIVITIES

• •

2 Put the sentences about Luke in order.

1 He picks up Westy's fur. ☐
2 He almost has a fight with Alex. ☐
3 He asks his mom to stay at home. ☐
4 He finds some animal tracks. ☐
5 He meets Alex before school. ☐ *1*
6 He burns the pizza. ☐
7 He sees Alex sitting on a wooden seat. ☐
8 He sits on his mom's bed. ☐

3 What do the <u>underlined</u> words refer to in these lines from the text?

1 I'd kept <u>it</u> to give to his owner, but I hadn't called him yet.
(page 38) ....*Westy's collar*....

2 I had cut <u>it</u> running through the trees the day before.
(page 38) ....

3 They stopped the sun from getting through and drying <u>it</u> out.
(page 40) ....

4 He was using <u>it</u> to cut into the seat. (page 42)

....

5 We'll do <u>it</u> tomorrow, OK? (page 45) ....

6 I threw <u>it</u> away. (page 46) ....

4 Match the two parts of the sentences.

1 Alex doesn't know [6]
2 Luke watched movies ☐
3 Alex is sitting ☐
4 Luke is very angry ☐
5 Luke's mom looks ☐
6 Jet runs back ☐

a on a wooden seat.
-b- about Jet.
c into the trees.
d with his dad.
e with Alex.
f at her watch.

5 Answer the questions.

1 Why does Luke know all about tracks in the ground?

2 What is Westy's owner's name?

3 Why doesn't Luke want his mom to go out?

4 Why doesn't Jet leave Ridge Woods?

LOOKING FORWARD

• •

6 Answer the questions.

1 Luke has a plan for Jet. What do you think it is?

2 Chapter 11 is called "Arguing." Who do you think argues?

Arguing

The next day, I got up an hour earlier than usual. I was very careful to be quiet so I didn't wake Mom. I dressed quickly in my school uniform and I didn't use the bathroom. Then I carried my school bag downstairs and went straight to the fridge. Seconds later, with the meat safely in my bag, I left the house.

There were lots of people walking their dogs up in Ridge Woods. Some of them said "Good morning" to me. But I didn't want to speak to anybody, so I mostly tried not to look at anyone.

I couldn't help looking at their dogs, though. There were black dogs and white dogs, big dogs and small dogs – dogs of all different colors and sizes. Some of the dogs played with dog toys and some of them chased birds. Some just walked quietly along with their owners. I knew that none of the dogs were safe with the big cat in Ridge Woods – not even the big ones. The cat needed to eat.

I didn't think the cat was bad. I thought that if I gave her meat, she wouldn't be hungry. I could get a part-time job so I had money to buy more meat for her. If I brought meat to Ridge Woods every day, the cat wouldn't need to kill any more dogs.

On my way to the soccer field, I had to walk past the poster on the tree about Westy. Two dog owners were talking to each other about it.

"It's terrible, isn't it?" one was saying.

"Phil's worried sick," the other one said. "That dog is everything to him."

I walked past with my head down.

I was very sorry Westy's owner was so sad. He was a nice man. But I knew I was doing something very important by taking the meat to the cat. Maybe that's why I didn't feel so afraid this time when I left the field and began to walk into the thick trees. I had come here to help the cat as well as to save the dogs. I thought the cat would know that.

Once again, there were no sounds in this part of the woods. Before, where the dog owners had been walking, birds were singing. There were no birds here. As I walked on, I was afraid again. I knew that the meat would smell very strong to the cat. My hands were shaking a little as I stopped to open my bag.

Suddenly there was a sound close by, like the sound of a stick being broken. I thought I saw eyes in the darkness, looking at me. My mouth went dry. I opened the bag and threw the meat down onto the ground. Then I walked backward through the trees toward the soccer field.

Everything was still, but I knew the cat was there. I knew it was waiting to eat the meat.

I didn't eat lunch that day. I kept the money. The last class of the day was gym. I told the teacher I didn't feel well and left school early. Then I went to the supermarket to buy some meat. I couldn't get much with the money I had and I hoped it would be enough.

When I got to Ridge Woods, I went straight to the part beyond the soccer field. Once again, everything was quiet and I tried not to make a sound as I walked through the trees. I knew the place where I had left the meat; it was close to two young silver birch trees. When I got there, the meat was gone and there were more large animal tracks on the ground. I knew the big cat had eaten the meat and I smiled. I got the fresh meat out of my bag and laid it down.

"I'll be back tomorrow," I whispered into the trees, where I knew she was hiding. Then I went home.

*   *   *

"This is nice, isn't it?" Mom said later.

We were sitting on the couch together, watching a DVD and eating hamburgers and fries. Mom had her feet up on the couch and she looked comfortable and happy. She had told me to choose the movie, but I had chosen one I knew she would like. I didn't care what we watched.

"It would be better if you put your shoes back on," I joked. "Your feet smell awful."

"I took a shower this morning!" Mom said. She made her voice sound angry, but I knew she wasn't really angry at all.

I laughed. "You need another one then!"

"What a terrible boy you are," Mom said, but she gave me a big smile as she said it.

I smiled back. I was feeling good. I thought the cat was probably asleep now. Big cats usually sleep after a meal, so any dogs in Ridge Woods would be safe. I was really happy about that.

It was good to laugh and joke with Mom again, too. When Dad was alive, we were always having fun. It didn't happen that often these days. Things could get a little too serious sometimes.

On the DVD, a family was sitting at a table eating dinner.

"What happened to the meat that was in the fridge?" Mom asked me suddenly.

Mom and I like to watch TV with the big light off, so I didn't think she could see the way my face turned red.

"I threw it away," I told her.

Mom looked at me. "Why in the world did you do that?" she asked.

"It smelled bad," I said. "I thought we might get sick."

"That's awful!" Mom said, sounding angry now. "I just bought it the other day. I was going to cook it tomorrow."

In the movie there was a sudden knock at the door, and a detective came in with a gun. The movie family screamed and Mom forgot about the meat.

I didn't though, because it made me remember that I had to buy more the next day. I wasn't sure how I was going to do that, since I didn't have any money. I could save my lunch money again, but I couldn't buy enough meat for the cat with just my lunch money.

"Have you seen much of Alex lately?" Mom asked me a little later.

I shook my head.

"No," I said. "Not much."

"Good," said Mom. "I don't like that boy. He's trouble."

I had kept away from Alex as much as possible today, but I knew it couldn't last. Alex would catch up with me sooner or later.

But I didn't want to think about Alex. Or to worry about how I was going to get more meat for the cat. I just wanted to enjoy the time with Mom.

But Mom didn't seem that interested in the movie anymore. She seemed to want to talk.

"I had a nice time last night," she said.

"The dinner was great. Interesting conversation, too." She waited for me to say something. When I didn't, she continued.

"I'd like you to meet Sam some time," she said. "He's the man I had dinner with. I met him a few months ago at work. He's a nice man. I think you'll like him."

I could feel my mouth like a hard line across my face. On the DVD someone was screaming again. I wanted to scream too – at Mom.

"Why did you have to say that? Why couldn't you just watch the DVD and let us have a nice time?" I thought.

Mom got up and put the light on. I think she wanted to see my face.

"Don't be like that, Luke," she said, sitting down again. Her voice sounded sad. "At least give him a chance."

I sat with my face turned toward the TV, but I wasn't watching it now and my hamburger and fries were getting cold.

"Your dad is gone, Luke," Mom told me softly. "He's never coming back."

That was just too much for me and I got up and ran to the door. My hamburger and fries fell onto the carpet, but I didn't care.

"Luke!" Mom called after me as I ran up the stairs. "Luke! I'm sorry, honey."

But I went into my room and closed the door, shutting out her voice.

*   *   *

I meant to get up early again the next day. I didn't want to see Alex and now I didn't want to see Mom, either. But I didn't sleep very well. All night I lay in bed thinking about Dad and feeling angry with Mom. It started to rain heavily some time during the night, too. I thought about the cat up in Ridge Woods in the rain, and hoped she was all right. It was still raining when I finally fell asleep in the early morning. Because I was so tired, I didn't wake up at the usual time. Mom had to wake me up.

"Luke," she said quietly, "it's after eight o'clock. Time to get up. You'll be late for school."

The sun was coming in through the windows. It hurt my eyes.

"Look," Mom said. "About last night ..."

I got quickly out of bed and walked away from her.

"I didn't mean to hurt you," Mom said, but I went into the bathroom and shut the door.

Mom came after me.

"Luke!" she said through the door. "You can't keep running away when you don't like what someone has to say. You're fourteen now, not four. It's time you began to act your age!"

I turned the shower on, hoping the noise of the water would shut out her voice. But all she said was, "I'll see you later, OK? We'll talk about this some more. I've got to go to work now."

I was late leaving for school, but Alex was still there, waiting for me.

"Been a busy boy lately, haven't you, Lukey?" he said. "Haven't seen you."

"Don't call me *Lukey*," I said angrily, trying to walk past him.

Alex took hold of my sweater and pulled me close.

"You don't tell *me* what to do!" he said.

His eyes looked wild and a little crazy. I was afraid he might hit me.

"Look," I said after a while, "we're friends, aren't we?"

Alex's eyes searched mine.

"I thought so," he said. "But now I'm not so sure. Friends spend time together."

"I've been a little fed up," I said. "That's all. I haven't felt like being with people."

"What do you have to be fed up about?" Alex asked, but he let go of my sweater and I knew that the danger was over. For now, at least.

"A few different things," I said, but Alex had already stopped listening.

It was the last day of school that day, and I thought about a whole summer with Alex. Alex wanting to start trouble. Alex wanting to start fires in Ridge Woods. I didn't know how I was going to get through it. Or how I was going to be able to keep the cat a secret.

Chapter 12

My dangerous friend

Everybody at school was very happy that day – even the teachers. Everybody except me. I felt as if I was watching everyone from a long way away, like in a dream. I didn't speak to anybody, so nobody spoke to me.

"What's wrong with him?" a boy in my math class asked Alex.

"He's fed up," Alex said in a loud voice and laughed as if it were a big joke.

At the end of the day, I hid in the boys' bathroom until everyone had gone. Then I went out to the parking lot and over the wall. I didn't see anybody I knew as I made my way to the supermarket.

I went straight to look at the meat. There was some that was half price. I looked at it. The "sell by" date was today, but it looked OK. I smiled as I went to pay, glad I could get more meat for my money.

It was the first time I'd felt happy all day. I had lots of food for the cat now. I just hoped she wasn't too hungry. It was twenty-four hours since her last meal.

I hurried up to Ridge Woods with the meat in my school bag. I was so impatient to be there, I didn't think about anything else. I certainly didn't see Alex following me. I didn't even realize he was there until after I'd left the soccer field and entered the woods.

When Alex called out to me, I jumped with surprise.

"Luke!"

I stopped to look at him.

"You made me jump," I said. "I didn't know you were there!"

"I know," said Alex happily. "I followed you all the way from school. You thought you could get away from me, didn't you? Going over the back wall like that. Had no idea I was behind you all the way up here."

Alex's face looked dangerous again. He took my school bag from me and began to open it.

"What did you buy at the supermarket? Some hot dogs to cook up here? Great idea. We can light a fire and throw them on!"

I didn't want him to get the meat out.

"Leave that alone," I said. "It's mine!"

"It's mine, it's mine!" Alex repeated in a baby voice. And he pulled the bag of meat out of my school bag.

"No!" I said. "Give it to me!"

Alex held the bag up high – too high for me to reach it. He was smiling all over his face.

"Get it from me if you want it so much," he said.

59

Suddenly I heard a noise – not a loud noise, just the sound of a stick breaking. It was so quiet, Alex didn't hear it. But I knew what it was.

"Go on," Alex was saying. "Get it from me!"

I looked over his shoulder and there she was. I saw her eyes first – her big, gold eyes. And then she came closer and I saw her body for the first time. She was *beautiful*. Long and deep black and very, very dangerous.

We looked at each other for several seconds, she and I. Then Alex began to open the bag of meat.

"Here!" he shouted at me. "If you want it so much, you can have it!" and he started to throw the meat at me.

Then everything happened at once. The panther began to move. I screamed at Alex to stop, be careful, I don't know what. Alex turned. He saw the panther just as she jumped. I'll never forget the look on his face. He was more than afraid – he was terrified. And then he began to scream …

I don't know how long Alex screamed for. Probably not long. I think I closed my eyes for a minute; I'm not sure. When I looked next, he was lying on the ground and the panther was gone.

"Alex!" I got down to look at him. There was blood on his sweater. I couldn't tell how bad it was, but I knew I needed to get help.

I stood up, looking around me. There was no one around. I didn't want to leave Alex to go for help. The panther might come back.

Then suddenly, I heard the sound of a phone. The sound was coming from Alex's pocket. And I remembered the phone he'd taken from the woman's bag; someone must be calling it. Hands shaking, I reached out to look in Alex's pocket. He was lying very still. I didn't know if he was alive or dead.

The phone stopped ringing just as I took it out of Alex's pocket. Quickly and carefully, I pressed 9-1-1. Then I put the phone to my ear.

"Emergency," said a voice on the other end. "Which service, please?"

Through the trees, I could see the panther's gold eyes watching me.

"Ambulance," I said. "A doctor. To Ridge Woods. My friend has … cut himself. I think … I think it's very serious."

The voice continued, asking me to describe better where we were. I did the best I could.

The voice on the phone asked me my name and told me help would arrive as soon as possible.

"All right," I said. "Thanks." Then I threw the phone down.

I knew help would arrive within minutes – five minutes at the most. And when they arrived, there would be lots of questions. I didn't want to look under Alex's sweater, but I knew if I did it would be clear what had happened. They would soon know about the cat. I had to help her. I didn't want them to catch her; they might kill her.

Alex made a little sound. He didn't wake up, but at least I knew he was alive.

"You'll be all right," I said to him. I don't think he could hear me, but I said it because I wanted to believe it myself. "You'll be all right. You'll be all right. Please be all right!" I wished.

I knew that if I had told someone about the cat right away, Alex wouldn't have been hurt. And now, because he *had* been hurt, the cat might be killed. It was all my fault.

I walked a short way away from Alex, toward those watching eyes.

"Run!" I told the cat loudly. "You have to run! They'll be here any minute. Please! Run!"

But she stayed where she was, watching me.

Alex made another sound. I went back over to him.

"Be quiet," I told him. "She might come back!" He didn't hear me.

I picked up the meat and threw it toward the cat to keep her busy. Then I saw a lighter that had fallen out of Alex's pocket. Fire! I could start a fire. Wild animals don't like fire; maybe it would frighten her away.

Working quickly, I began to pick up sticks. I put them all together and then I reached into my bag for one of my schoolbooks and began to take the pages out. I put the paper with the wood and then I picked up Alex's lighter. I lit it and held it to the paper. Then I heard the sound of the ambulance; they were coming. The paper caught fire quickly, but the sticks were wet from the rain and only made smoke.

"Please," I said. "*Please.*"

The ambulance was very close now. I tried blowing on the sticks and the paper to help them catch fire, but it only made more smoke. I tried the lighter again, but it was no good.

Behind me, the ambulance had stopped. I could hear voices shouting to me from the soccer field.

"Hello? Luke? Where are you?"

Alex made another noise. I quickly stepped on the sticks and paper to hide what I had been trying to do.

I looked toward the cat, but she had gone.

"Over here!" I shouted. "We're over here!"

There were two men. They came running quickly through the trees toward us. As soon as they arrived, they got down on the ground and began working on Alex.

"What's his name?" the taller one asked me.

He had taken a large pair of scissors[13] from his bag and now he was cutting Alex's sweater off.

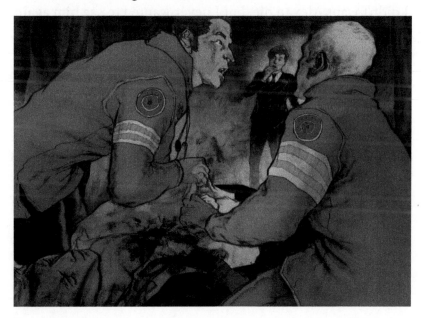

"Alex," I said, turning away quickly. But it was too late; I had seen the blood on Alex's body and I threw up on the ground.

"Alex," the shorter man was saying. "Can you hear me, Alex?"

Alex made another sound.

"We're going to get you to the hospital in a minute," the shorter man told him.

"How did this happen, Luke?" the taller man asked me, but I just held my stomach and shook my head.

Then I threw up again.

"Are you all right, Luke?" the taller man asked me. "Are you hurt at all?"

"No," I said. "I'm all right."

I knew they would discover the truth somehow. They would guess, or Alex would tell them. But *I* didn't want to tell them. The cat was my friend; Alex wasn't. The cat had tried to help me. All Alex did was try to hurt me or get me into trouble. I didn't want Alex to die, but I never wanted to see him again.

"The cuts don't look deep," the taller ambulance man said. "But he's lost some blood. Let's take him to the hospital."

The men put Alex carefully onto a stretcher[14] and then they looked at me.

"Come on, Luke," they said.

I knew I had to go with them; I had no choice. As we walked away toward the ambulance, I looked around one last time for the cat. But I still couldn't see her.

I thought I'd never see her again. "Good-bye," I said in my head. "Good-bye."

When we got to the hospital, the police were waiting to talk to me.

LOOKING BACK

● ●

1 Check your answers to *Looking forward* on page 49.

ACTIVITIES

● ●

2 Are the sentences true (*T*) or false (*F*)?

1 Luke thinks the cat will stop killing if he gives it meat. ☐ T
2 Luke doesn't have lunch because he doesn't feel well. ☐
3 Luke and his mom don't have much fun these days. ☐
4 The meat in the fridge was bad. ☐
5 Luke doesn't want to meet his mom's new friend. ☐
6 Luke buys some cheap meat. ☐
7 Jet disappears after she jumps on Alex. ☐
8 Luke doesn't want to be Alex's friend anymore. ☐

3 Match the two parts of the sentences.

1 Luke doesn't use the bathroom because ☐ b
2 Luke doesn't have lunch because ☐
3 Luke turns the shower on because ☐
4 Luke doesn't see Alex following him because ☐
5 Luke doesn't want anyone to catch Jet because ☐
6 Luke doesn't want to see Alex again because ☐

a he wants the money to buy meat for Jet.
b he doesn't want to wake his mom.
c he gets him into trouble.
d he doesn't want to listen to his mom.
e they might kill her.
f he is thinking about Jet.

4 **Read the sentences from the text and answer the questions.**

1 I could feel my mouth like a hard line across my face. (page 55) How do you think Luke is feeling here?

....

2 "Friends spend time together." (page 57) What is Alex saying here?

....

3 It was all my fault. (page 62) Why does Luke feel bad?

....

5 **Answer the questions.**

1 Why does Luke think about getting a part-time job?

....

2 Who is Sam?

....

3 Why doesn't Luke sleep well that night?

....

4 Why does Jet attack Alex?

....

5 Why does Luke try to start a fire?

....

LOOKING FORWARD

6 **What do you think happens in the final chapters?**

1 The police look for Jet and ....

....

2 Luke and his mom ....

....

Chapter 13

Talking to Mom

They called our mothers right away. Mrs. Brown was in with Alex now. Uncle Rob was with her.

"Alex!" Mrs. Brown had screamed when she arrived. "Alex, my Alex! What have they done to you?" Then a nurse closed the door.

A policewoman was sitting with me. There was a policeman, too. He wanted to ask me some questions, but we had to wait for Mom to get here first. She was on her way to the hospital from work.

The hospital was busy. Phones rang. Nurses and doctors kept walking past. I wanted Mom to arrive. It seemed like ages since they'd called her.

"Can I get you a drink, Luke?" the policeman asked me kindly, but I just shook my head. I didn't want to speak.

"Luke!"

Suddenly Mom was there, walking quickly toward me. Her face looked worried.

"Mom!"

She sat down beside me and held me in her arms like a little kid.

"What's all this?" she said. "What's happened?"

"It's my fault," I said. "It's all my fault." And I began to cry.

I wasn't just crying about Alex and the cat. I was crying about Dad too, and about feeling so alone. Mom and I had waited at this same hospital three years ago while Dad slowly died.

We were friends, Dad and me. We went to soccer games together. We played computer games together. I could talk to him about anything and I missed him so much it hurt. That's why the cat had been so special – she had been mine, my secret. I knew I had been wrong to keep quiet about her, but I hadn't wanted to lose her.

"I'll find us an office to use, Mrs. Robinson," I heard the policeman say. "We need to talk."

"All right," Mom answered him and then she spoke softly to me. "It's all right, honey. Everything will be all right."

Slowly, I stopped crying. When I sat back, Mom handed me a handkerchief. I blew my nose. Then the policeman came back.

"If you'd like to come this way?" he asked.

Mom stood up.

"Come on, Luke, honey," she said.

It was a small office for four people. I sat down beside Mom and, although I didn't look up, I could feel everyone looking at me.

"OK, Luke," the policeman said, "I'd like you to tell us what happened up in Ridge Woods; how Alex got hurt. It's very important that you tell us the truth and that you tell us everything."

I didn't speak right away.

Mom put her hand on my arm.

"Come on, honey," she said. "You won't get into trouble."

I looked up at the policeman's face and I wasn't so sure she was right about that. He looked very serious. But I wasn't worried about getting into trouble. I just wanted this to be all over. I wanted the cat to be safe too, but I didn't want anybody else to get hurt.

"There ... There's a cat up in Ridge Woods," I said at last. "A big cat. A black panther."

Mom made a sound. "A *panther*?" she said.

"This isn't just a story, is it Luke?" the policeman asked.

"No!" I said angrily. "It's the truth. I first saw her three days ago. She ... She killed a dog. Westy. I ... I've been taking her meat so she wouldn't kill anything else. Then, today ... Alex and I were fighting. She jumped on him to help me."

The policeman stood up and began to walk toward the door. He looked at Mom.

"I have to tell them about the cat," he said. "I'll be back to speak to your son soon."

"They won't hurt her, will they?" I asked him, but he was already on his way out of the door.

"Please don't hurt her!" I shouted, but it was too late; he had gone.

I was almost crying again.

"I don't want them to kill her," I told Mom.

"I'm sure they won't unless they really have to," she said and then she shook her head. "I can't believe all this," she told me. "I just can't believe it. You've been up there day after day with a dangerous cat. You've taken it *meat*! You could have been killed, Luke!"

My face was wet again.

"Don't be mad at me," I said.

Mom took me in her arms.

"Oh, Luke," she said, "I'm not mad at you. I just feel *sick* at the thought of it. All this time you were in danger, and I didn't know. I was too busy going out with the girls and on dates."

The policewoman got up.

"I'll come back in fifteen minutes," she told us gently and she went out, closing the door quietly behind her.

"I'm so sorry, Luke," Mom said. She was crying too now, and for a while we just held each other.

"I felt like you didn't care what I did," I told her after a few minutes. "You're always so busy."

Mom blew her nose.

"I *am* busy," she told me. "And I don't see that changing much, Luke. There's only me earning any money with your dad gone. But if you think I don't care about you, then you're wrong." She held my hands and looked into my face. "I care about you more than anything or anyone, and I always will."

I looked back at her.

"What about this Sam?" I asked.

"That's different," she said. "Sam's a nice man. A good man. I'm sure I will see him again. Maybe something will happen between us and maybe it won't. Look, Luke, nobody will ever take the place of your dad. You've got to believe that. But I'm still a young woman – he wouldn't have wanted me to be alone all my life."

I knew it was true. Dad had loved Mom very much. He would want her to be happy.

"But if I see Sam or not, *you'll* always be most important to me. Understood?"

I gave her a small smile.

"Yes," I said.

"But you have to talk to me, Luke," she went on. "You have to tell me how you're feeling about things. I can't help if I don't know."

"I'll try," I said and then I looked at her. "Can we move, Mom?" I asked her. "Can we move to another part of town?" I wanted to get away from Alex, but I didn't like to say that – not with him lying in a hospital bed a few meters away.

"Move?" Mom said. "Why do you want to move, honey?"

I looked down at our hands.

"I'd like … I'd like to go to a different school," I said.

When I looked up at her, she was smiling and I knew she understood.

"We'll see, honey," she said.

"*Please.*" I said.

"We'll think about it, Luke," she said.

The door opened again. It was the policewoman. She was smiling.

"Good news," she said.

I thought she was going to say that they had caught the panther alive. That she was OK and they were going to find a safe, new home for her.

"Your friend Alex is awake. He's going to be all right."

"Oh," I said.

"He's asking for you," the policewoman continued. "Do you want to go and see him before we talk?"

I thought about the look on Alex's face as he'd thrown the meat at me. I remembered his crazy dancing as the trees had burned in Ridge Woods.

"No," I said. "No, I don't want to see him."

Chapter 14

Home

Jet left Ridge Woods as quickly and as quietly as she had arrived, keeping to trees when she could and walking along the sides of dark fields when she couldn't. In one field she found some cows. She killed one and ate well. Afterward, she wanted to sleep, but she didn't. She had to make the best use she could of the dark.

The sun was almost up when Jet stopped again. It wasn't food that had stopped her this time; it was a smell. A strong smell that made her beautiful black body light up inside. It was the smell of other panthers – her own kind.

Chapter 15

Writing again

It wasn't just in the newspaper. The story of the black panther caught outside a zoo[15] in the country was on the TV.

I knew it was her, even before I saw pictures of her on TV. Even before journalists started knocking on our front door for my story, I knew.

Mom helped me talk to the newspapers. I'm going to write the story myself for one of the papers. They're going to pay me for it. We're moving soon; I'll use the money from the story to help Mom with our new house. And if there's enough, I'll give some to the zoo to pay them to take care of Jet.

That's what I told the zoo people she was called. I don't know why; it just seemed right.

LOOKING BACK

· ·

1 Check your answers to *Looking forward* on page 67.

ACTIVITIES

· ·

2 <u>Underline</u> the correct words in each sentence.

1 Luke is waiting at the hospital with *Mrs. Brown* / <u>*a policewoman*</u>.

2 Luke's mom *is* / *isn't* mad at him.

3 The policewoman leaves the room to *tell someone about the cat* / *leave Luke and his mom to talk*.

4 Luke's mom will continue to be busy because she *has to work* / *wants to go out with the girls*.

5 Luke thinks that his dad *would* / *wouldn't* be happy for his mom to go out with Sam.

6 Luke's mom *understands* / *doesn't understand* why he wants to go to a new school.

7 Jet doesn't sleep because she *wants to walk while it is dark* / *is hungry*.

3 Are the sentences true (*T*) or false (*F*)?

1 There are a lot of people at the hospital. ☐ T

2 Luke's mom is waiting at the hospital when he arrives. ☐

3 Luke doesn't have a drink. ☐

4 At first, the policeman isn't sure if Luke is telling the truth. ☐

5 Luke's mom loves him more than she loves Sam. ☐

6 Luke is very happy when the policewoman tells him that Alex is OK. ☐

7 Luke gives Jet her name. ☐

4 Match the two parts of the sentences.

1 Mrs. Brown is the first to $\boxed{e}$
2 The policeman wants to $\square$
3 Luke is worried that Jet is going to $\square$
4 Luke's mom is going to $\square$
5 Luke wants to $\square$
6 Luke doesn't want to $\square$
7 At the zoo, Jet can $\square$

a see Sam again.
b smell other panthers.
c die.
d visit Alex.
e arrive at the hospital.
f get away from Alex.
g talk to Luke.

5 Answer the questions.

1 Why is Luke thinking about his dad at the hospital?

....

2 Why does the policeman leave the room?

....

3 Why does Luke want to move to a new house?

....

4 Do you think Jet is happy in the end?

....

5 Why does Luke call the panther Jet?

....

Glossary

[1]**roar** (page 11) *verb*   to make a loud, deep sound

[2]**throat** (page 11) *noun*   the back part of your mouth and the part inside your neck

[3]**tight** (page 13) *adverb*   firmly, in a way that is difficult to move

[4]**guess** (page 21) *verb*   to think something is true when you don't have all the facts and cannot be certain if you are correct

[5]**whole** (page 26) *adjective*   complete, including every part

[6]**couple** (page 31) *noun*   two people who are married or are boyfriend and girlfriend

[7]**not unless** (page 34) *conjunction*   only if

[8]**bang** (page 39) *noun/exclamation*   a sudden loud noise; (here) the noise a child makes when playing with a gun

[9]**chest** (page 42) *noun*   the front of your body between your neck and your stomach

[10]**path** (page 42) *noun*   a long, thin area of ground for people to walk along

[11]**oven** (page 45) *noun*   the part of a stove with a door that you use for cooking food

[12]**bright** (page 47) *adjective*   full of light, shining

[13]**(pair of) scissors** (page 63) *noun*   an object used for cutting paper, cloth, etc. that you hold in your hand

[14]**stretcher** (page 64) *noun*   a flat object that is used to carry someone who is very sick or hurt

[15]**zoo** (page 77) *noun*   a place where animals are kept and people go to look at them